SUPER BOWL CHAMPIONS
GREEN BAY PACKERS

WIDE RECEIVER JAMES JONES

Published by Creative Education
P.O. Box 227, Mankato, Minnesota 56002
Creative Education is an imprint of The Creative Company
www.thecreativecompany.us

Design and production by Blue Design
Art direction by Rita Marshall
Printed in the United States of America

Photographs by AP Images (AP Photo/Pro Football
Hall of Fame), Getty Images (Lee Balterman/Sports
Illustrated, James V. Biever, MATT CAMPBELL/AFP, Tom
Dahlin, Jonathan Daniel, Stephen Dunn, Jeff Gross, Al
Messerschmidt, Darryl Norenberg, Pro Football Hall of
Fame, Frank Rippon/NFL, Gregory Shamus, David Stluka)

Library of Congress Cataloging-in-Publication Data
Frisch, Aaron.
Green Bay Packers / Aaron Frisch.
p. cm. — (Super bowl champions)
Includes index.
Summary: An elementary look at the Green Bay Packers
professional football team, including its formation in 1919,
most memorable players, Super Bowl championships, and
stars of today.
ISBN 978-1-60818-376-0
1. Green Bay Packers (Football team)—History—Juvenile
literature. I. Title.

GV956.G7F75 2014
796.332'640977561—dc23   2013010565

First Edition
9 8 7 6 5 4 3 2 1

LAMBEAU LEAP

CLARK HINKLE / 1932–41

Clark was a fullback who scored a lot of touchdowns. Green Bay was the only team he played for.

TABLE OF CONTENTS

BART STARR / 1956–71
Bart was the NFL's best quarterback in the 1960s. He was smart and threw **accurate** passes.

NITSCHKE: *NITCH-kee*

ONE OF THE FIRST TEAMS

In 1919, a football team formed in Green Bay, Wisconsin. A meat-packing company gave it uniforms. To thank the company, the players called themselves the Packers!

RAY NITSCHKE / 1958–72

Ray was a fierce linebacker who led the Packers' defense in the 1960s with his rough tackles.

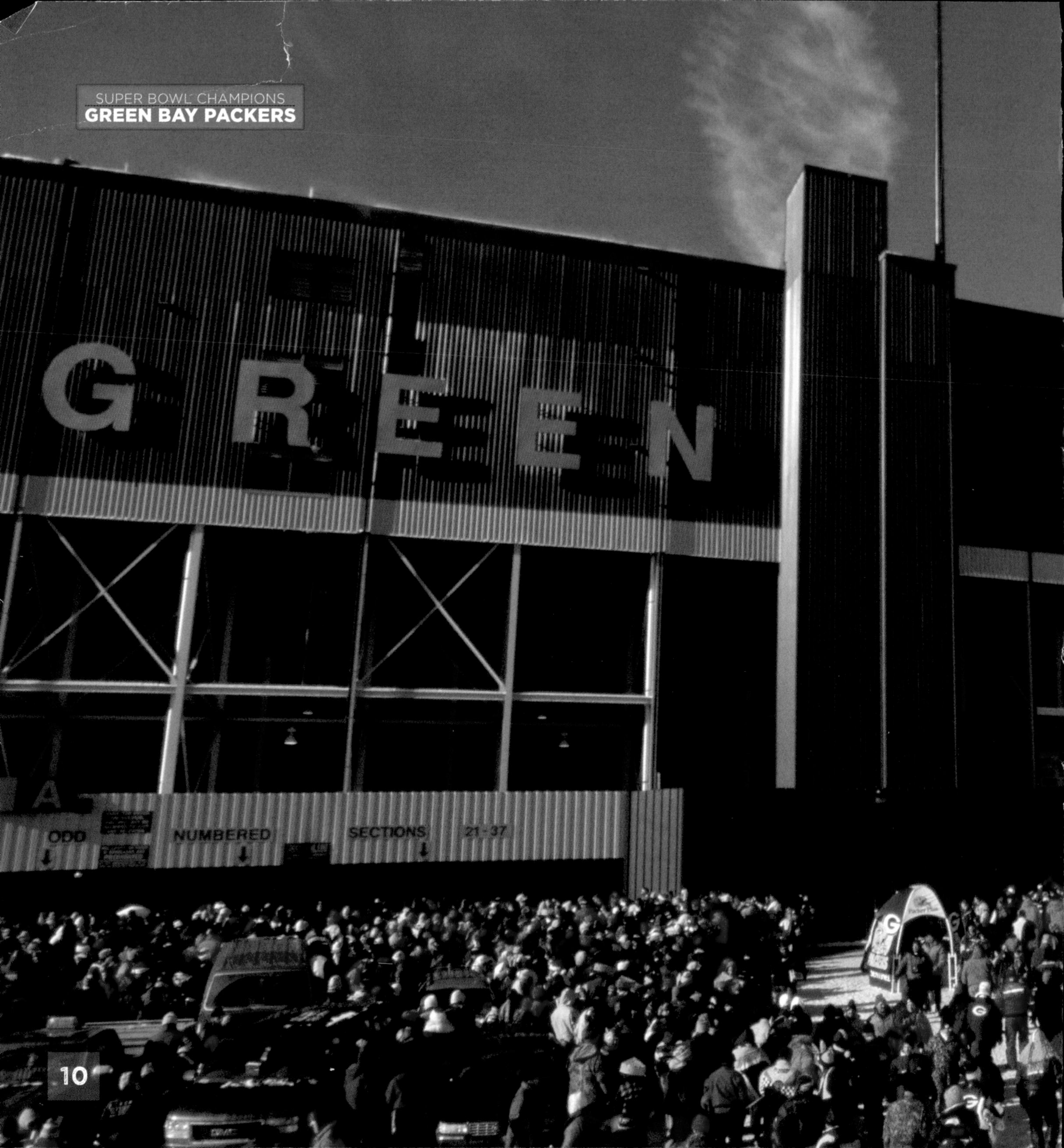
GREEN
ODD
NUMBERED
SECTIONS
21 - 37

WELCOME TO GREEN BAY

About 100,000 people live in Green Bay. It is the smallest city with a National Football League (NFL) team. Winters can be very cold in Green Bay.

STERLING SHARPE / 1988-94

Sterling was a wide receiver who was both fast and powerful. He played in the Pro Bowl five times.

TITLETOWN U.S.A.

By 2013, the Packers had won 13 NFL championships. This is why people call Green Bay "Titletown U.S.A."! ("Title" is another word for championship.)

WIDE RECEIVER JORDY NELSON

"For every pass I caught in a game, I caught a thousand in practice."

—DON HUTSON

THE PACKERS' STORY

The Packers played their first season in 1919. Curly Lambeau coached the team and played running back. The Packers became NFL champions in 1929, 1930, and 1931.

In 1933, the Packers added fast wide receiver Don Hutson. He helped Green Bay win three more championships in 1936, 1939, and 1944.

CURLY LAMBEAU

15

VINCE LOMBARDI

SOUND IT OUT

LOMBARDI: *lom-BAR-dee*

The Packers hired a coach named Vince Lombardi in 1959. After the 1966 and 1967 seasons, Coach Lombardi's Packers won the first two Super Bowls ever played.

REGGIE WHITE / 1993–98

Reggie was a 300-pound defensive end. He made almost 200 sacks while playing in the NFL.

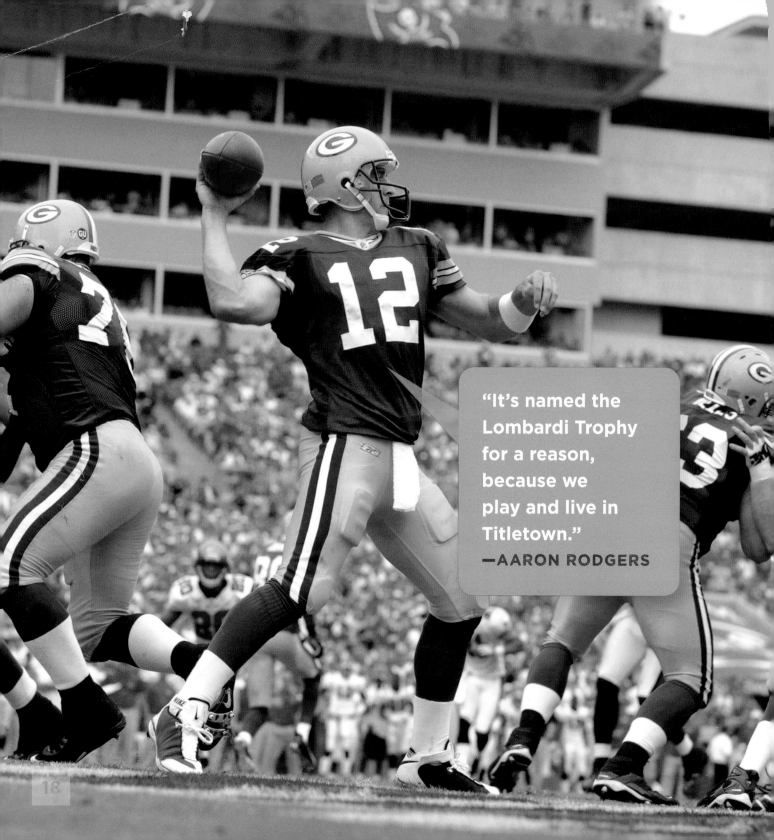

"It's named the Lombardi Trophy for a reason, because we play and live in Titletown."

—AARON RODGERS

BRETT FAVRE

It took a long time for the Packers to become great again. In the 1990s, quarterback Brett Favre was fun to watch. He led the Packers to victory in Super Bowl XXXI (31).

Aaron Rodgers replaced Brett as quarterback in 2008. Aaron threw passes to a lot of speedy receivers. After the 2010 season, the Packers won the Super Bowl again.

CHARLES WOODSON / 2006–12

Charles was a cornerback who made many interceptions. He was an important team leader.

F ast linebacker Clay Matthews led a tough Packers defense in 2013. Clay and his teammates worked hard to bring more titles to Titletown U.S.A.!

CLAY MATTHEWS

21

FACTS FILE

CONFERENCE/DIVISION:
National Football
Conference, North Division

TEAM COLORS:
Green and yellow

HOME STADIUM:
Lambeau Field

SUPER BOWL VICTORIES:
I, January 15, 1967 / 35–10
  over Kansas City Chiefs
II, January 14, 1968 / 33–14
  over Oakland Raiders
XXXI, January 26, 1997 /
  35–21 over New England
  Patriots
XLV, February 6, 2011 / 31–
  25 over Pittsburgh Steelers

NFL WEBSITE FOR KIDS:
http://nflrush.com

WIDE RECEIVER
GREG JENNINGS

23

GLOSSARY

accurate — on target, or right where something needs to be

interceptions — plays in which a defensive player catches a pass thrown by the other team

Pro Bowl — a special game after the season that only the best NFL players get to play

sacks — plays in which a defensive player tackles a quarterback who is trying to throw a pass

---

INDEX